Bead-tube jewelry is made using a mix of crochet and beading.

The technique is much easier to do than it looks. All crocheted bead-tube is worked the same way; the only difference is how many beads you choose to use in each round. In *How to Crochet Bead-Tube Jewelry*, you will find a Getting Started DVD that includes beading information, plus an actual demonstration on making a five-bead tube. If you would like to practice along with the DVD, the instructions for the tube can be found on page 3. We've also included a Beading Basics section to answer all your questions on bead types, findings, tools and finishing your pieces. So gather your materials and start stitching today!

HOW TO CROCHET
bead-tube
JEWELRY™

With
Getting
Started
DVD

Table of Contents

Bead-Tube Crochet 3

Special Stitches 4

Beading Guide 7

    Bead Sizes 7

    Average Jewelry Lengths 7

    Bead Quantity Table 7

    Bead Types 8

    Finding Types 10

    Tools & Supplies 13

Beading Basics How-to Guide 16

    Make Your Own Basic Clasp......... 16

    Bead Caps 16

    Crimping.............................. 17

    Crimp Covers 18

    Opening & Closing Jump Rings ... 18

    Making Your Own Jump Rings 18

    4-in-1 Pliers 19

    Knots 20

    Simple Loops 21

Projects 22

    Black & Silver Affair ... 22

    Colors of Autumn 27

    Flower Vine Set 31

    Shades of Nature 37

    Chunky
    Bronzite & Gold 41

    Gold & Bronze Set...... 43

Crochet Stitch Guide **47**

Bead-Tube Crochet

All bead-tube crochet is worked in the same way. The only difference is how many beads you decide to use per round.

Be sure to thread your beads onto the thread before beginning the project. Always string the beads in reverse order.

If you are alternating between three or more bead colors, you will notice that when inserting your hook in the stitch to pull up another bead that the bead already in stitch and the one that you are pulling up are always the same color. This will happen with each "pair" of beads.

When inserting your hook into the stitch that has a bead, be sure that the bead is to the right of your hook. When pulling up a bead, always pull it to the right of the hook.

Use some thread conditioner or beeswax before threading, or you can use a beading needle to thread beads on the yarn.

You will chain 1 more than beads used as follows:

3 beads………chain 4

4 beads………chain 5

5 beads………chain 6

6 beads………chain 7

7 beads………chain 8

8 beads………chain 9

9 beads………chain 10

The extra chain is used for joining the first round.

You may want to make a practice swatch using yarn and pony beads until you feel confident, and then move on to thread and seed beads.

The swatch in the video is made with five different colors of pony beads and yarn. Work 10 rounds of bead tube plus the last rnd.

The basic crocheted bead tube is worked with a five-bead pattern as follows:

BEAD-TUBE CROCHET FOR SWATCH

Slide the threaded beads for your pattern up to a comfortable distance to the work area.

Rnd 1: Ch 6, join with sl st in **back lp** (see Stitch Guide) of first ch to form ring, **bead sl st** (see Special Stitches on page 4) in next ch and in each ch around, **do not join rnds**.

The beads on rnd 1 will be lying horizontally. Their orientation will change to stand vertically as rnd 2 is worked.

Rnd 2: Bead sl st in same st as bead on last rnd, making sure your thread is in front of previous-row bead and your thread is to the right of hook, bead sl st in each st around.

Rnds 3–10: Rep rnd 2 until you have the amount of rnds you need for your pattern.

After stitching several rnds, you will see how the woven effect of this technique creates the bead tube. Also notice how the beads begin to spiral up the tube.

Last rnd: Sl st in each st around. Fasten off.

The beads on the last rnd will stand up vertically. ∎

TIP If you look at the side of the tube and a bead seems to be receding or is in the center of the tube, it means that the bead you moved to the right of the hook has slipped through as you pulled the loop through the loops on the hook, or perhaps, the wrapped thread did not come from the right of the bead on the hook. If this happens, you can try to push the bead back out again. If you are unable to do so, you need to pull out stitches until your work looks correct again.

Special Stitches

Photos are shown using yarn and pony beads in order to make it easier to see.

SPECIAL STITCHES

Bead slip stitch (bead sl st): Insert hook in **back lp** *(see Stitch Guide)* of ch or st as indicated *(see Photo A)*, pull up bead, yo, pull lp through ch or st and lp on hook *(see Photo B)*.

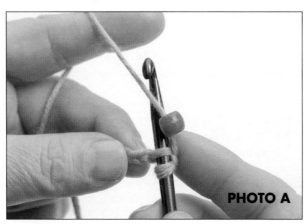

PHOTO A

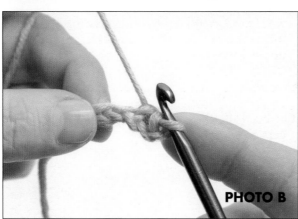

PHOTO B

Bead single crochet (bead sc): Insert hook in **back lp** *(see Stitch Guide)* of st as indicated *(see Photo C)*, pull up bead, yo, pull through st, yo, pull through all lps on hook *(see Photos D and E)*.

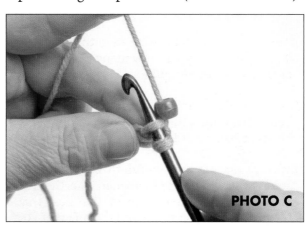

PHOTO C

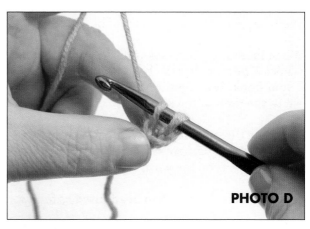

PHOTO D

PHOTO E

Bead half double crochet (bead hdc): Yo, insert hook in **back lp** *(see Stitch Guide)* of st as indicated *(see Photo F)*, pull up bead, yo, pull through st and 2 lps on hook *(see Photo G)*.

Bead double crochet (bead dc): Yo, insert hook in **back lp** *(see Stitch Guide)* of st as indicated, pull up bead *(see Photo H)*, yo, pull through st and first lp on hook, pull up bead *(see Photo I)*, yo, pull through last 2 lps on hook *(see Photo J)*.

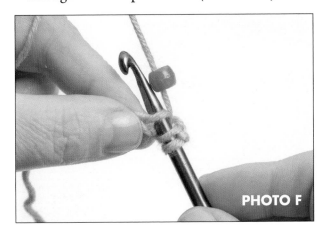

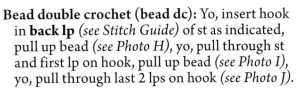

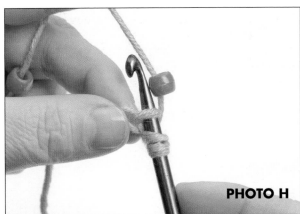

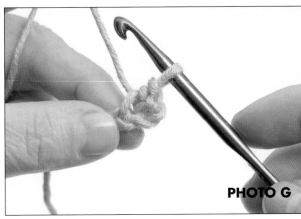

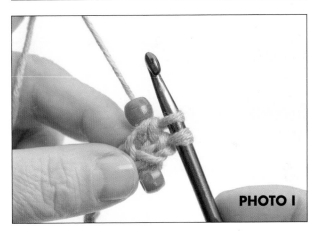

Bead double double crochet (bead double dc):
Yo 3 times *(see Photo K)*, insert hook in **back
lp** *(see Stitch Guide)* of st as indicated, pull up
bead, yo, pull through st and first lp on hook,
[pull up bead, yo, pull through 2 lps on hook]
3 times *(see Photos L–P)*.

PHOTO N

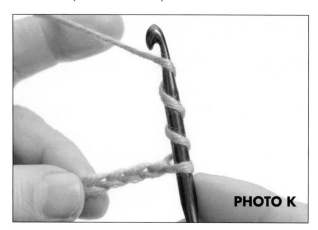

PHOTO K

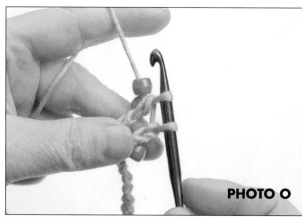

PHOTO O

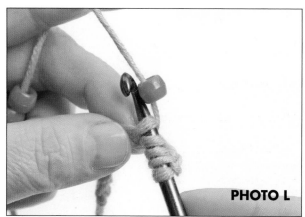

PHOTO L

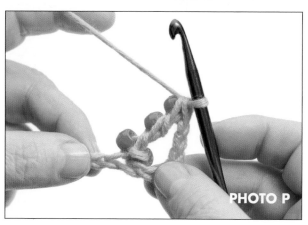

PHOTO P

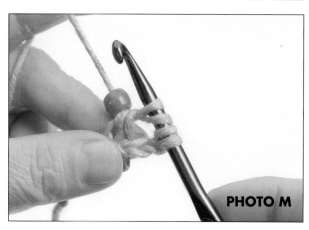

PHOTO M

Beading Guide

This handy beading guide is jam-packed with helpful information about beading. You will find photos and step-by-step illustrations for bead types, findings and tools. Whether you are a beginner or an experienced crocheter, you will use this reference guide again and again.

BEAD SIZES

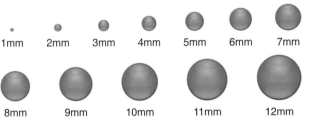

1mm 2mm 3mm 4mm 5mm 6mm 7mm

8mm 9mm 10mm 11mm 12mm

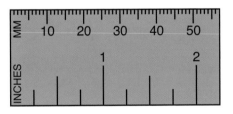

BEAD QUANTITY TABLE

Use this simple table to estimate the number of beads per inch.

BEAD	APPROXIMATE BEADS PER INCH
#11 seed bead	12–14
#8 seed bead	8
#6 seed bead	6
2mm bead	12
4mm bead	6
6mm bead	4
8mm bead	3
10mm bead	2
12mm bead	2

AVERAGE JEWELRY LENGTHS

Bracelet	7 inches
Anklet	9 inches
Choker	16 inches
Princess length	18 inches
Matinee length	24 inches
Opera length	32 inches
Rope or lariat	48 inches

BEAD TYPES

ACRYLIC BEADS

Available in a variety of beautiful colors and shapes, acrylic beads offer an economical and lightweight alternative to glass beads.

GLASS BEADS

Glass beads are a broad category of beads, including art glass, cane glass, cat's-eye, chevron, crackle glass, faceted, lampwork, crow, cubic zirconia, dichroic glass and foil-lined glass.

E BEADS

A part of the seed-bead category, this size 6/0 or 8/0 bead is often referred to as an E bead, and will add color and interest to your beading projects.

METAL BEADS

From sterling silver to copper, shiny to antique, metal beads are available in a variety of finishes, shapes and sizes to match your every design.

PEARLS

Whether cultured, freshwater, crystal or glass, pearls add a touch of sophistication to your jewelry designs. The versatility of pearls allows them to be styled in both elegant and contemporary designs. Real pearls vary slightly in color, shape and size.

SEED BEADS

Seed beads are the most widely used beads in jewelry design; these beads can be used as filler beads, woven into designs or used to create intricate patterns and shapes. The most common sizes are 11/0 and 15/0—the larger the number, the smaller the bead.

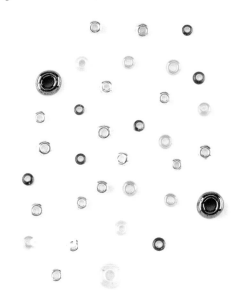

PENDANTS

Pendants change the look of your design immediately. Add them to your favorite necklace or incorporate them into your design from the beginning.

FINDING TYPES

Findings are additional supplies or tools needed to make your jewelry.

BEAD CAPS
Bead caps add flair and dimension to your bead projects and come in a wide variety of sizes, shapes and finishes to accommodate all your design ideas. They can also be used to serve as protection between beads.

CLASPS
Claps not only secure your beading projects, they can become part of the design as well. Clasps are available in bar and ring toggles, barrel, bead, box, button, filigree, fishhook, hook-and-eye, lobster-claw, magnetic, multistrand, S-hook, slide lock, spring-ring, snap lock and tube.

CHAIN
Perk up your projects with a beautiful chain. Available in large- to small-shaped links, rope, serpentine, figaro, flat and cable, to name a few, chain adds sparkle to your projects and comes in many finishes to coordinate with your beads and other findings.

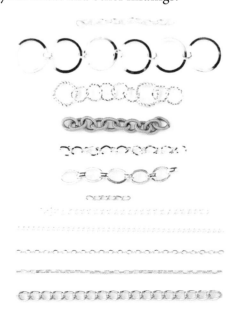

CRIMP BEADS & TUBES
Crimps are used at the beginning and end of your beading wire or thread to secure a clasp. They come in a bead or tube shape, and can even come with a ring attached.

CRIMP-BEAD COVERS

Crimp-bead covers disguise and protect your crimp beads. They blend into the strand of beads, giving your designs a finished, professional look.

EARRING FINDINGS

Earring findings are available in a variety of styles, sizes and finishes to complement your every design. Options include ear studs, hook ear wires, ear threads, hoop earrings, lever-back, clip-on, half-ball post, ball post and chandelier.

EYE PINS

A straight pin with the eye already created for you, eye pins give you endless design possibilities.

HEAD PINS

A straight pin with a flattened end, this versatile pin allows you to create many different designs in necklaces, earrings and bracelets.

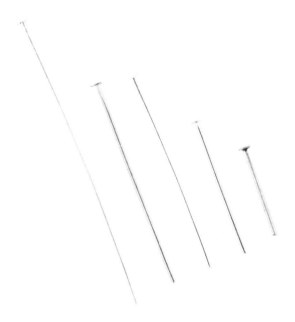

JUMP RINGS

Jump rings are not just for holding your necklace together. Now jump rings are being used in a variety of ways to add dimension and design possibilities. They can also be weaved into chain maille.

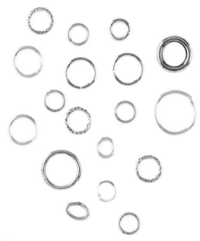

SPACER BARS

Spacer bars are invaluable when creating multistranded pieces. They help keep your wire separated for a great look.

SPLIT RINGS

Not just for key chains, these double jump rings offer more security for your precious gems and stores.

LINKS

Links come in every style and color, from plain to very fancy. Use links to connect pieces of your design or to add a bit of whimsy or interest.

Beading findings such as eye pins, head pins and jump rings are made from wires of different gauges and harnesses. Gauges of wire come in a variety of sizes, 18–26 for example; the smaller the number, the larger the gauge and vice versa.

TOOLS & SUPPLIES

BEAD MAT

This is a small velour mat designed to keep your beads from rolling off your worktable.

BEAD DESIGN BOARD

A flocked board with grooves, it is used to lay out your beads and aid in your design. It contains small, shallow compartments for beads and findings.

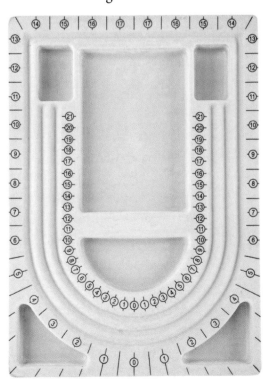

BEAD REAMER

A bead reamer is used to smooth rough edges on beads and to straighten or enlarge drilled holes in beads.

BEADING NEEDLES

This small, thin wire needle has a large flexible eye for threads, cords and various stringing items. Eyes vary in size; the higher the number, the smaller the needle. Some beading needles also resemble traditional needles. Sizes 10–15 are generally used for bead stitches.

BEADING-WIRE CUTTERS

Also known as flush cutters, these cutters are used to cut flexible beading wire. They have a thin, pointed tip that can get in between beads to trim wire ends. Do not use to cut normal wires because it will damage the cutting edges.

GLUE

Various glues can be used to secure knots, glue beads onto illusion cord and add end beads to memory wire. For jewelry, you want glue that dries soft or flexible, and that is not brittle.

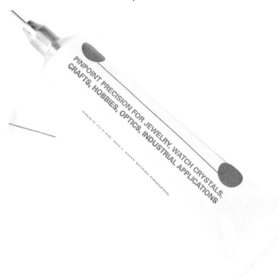

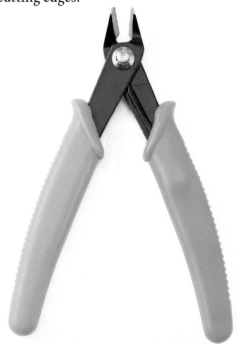

THREAD CONDITIONER

Beeswax keeps your thread from fraying, helps to protect it from moisture and decay, allows your beads to slide easily, and helps create tighter stitches.

GAUGE TOOL

There is no more guessing at the gauge of your wire or the size of your beads. Use this handy little tool to get an accurate measurement every time.

PLIERS

4-IN-1

This tool is named because of its four
functions: manipulating, flattening,
closing and cutting.

BENT-NOSE

The bend in the nose of these pliers makes
them useful in hard-to-reach places.

CHAIN-NOSE

Flat on the inside and rounded on the
outside, these pliers are used to create
90-degree bends in wire using the flat
surfaces and rounded bends when wire is
wrapped over the top portion of the jaws.
They are commonly used to work in tight
places or to open jump rings. Chain-nose
pliers differ from flat-nose because they
have a smaller, pointed tip.

CRIMP

These specialized pliers are used to close and
fold crimp beads and tubes. The back slot
makes a C-shaped dent in the crimp bead,
and the front slot rounds the crimp bead for
a professional look.

END-CUTTING

These basic work pliers can be used to cut
head pins, wire and a variety of jewelry-
making items.

FLAT-NOSE

Flat-nose pliers have a smooth jaw that is
used to grip, bend and flatten wire without
marking it.

LOOP-CLOSING

These specialty pliers have a groove on the
top and bottom jaw to smoothly close jump
rings without distorting or scratching.

SPLIT-RING OPENING

These specialty pliers allow you to open any
size split ring with ease so attachments can
be added.

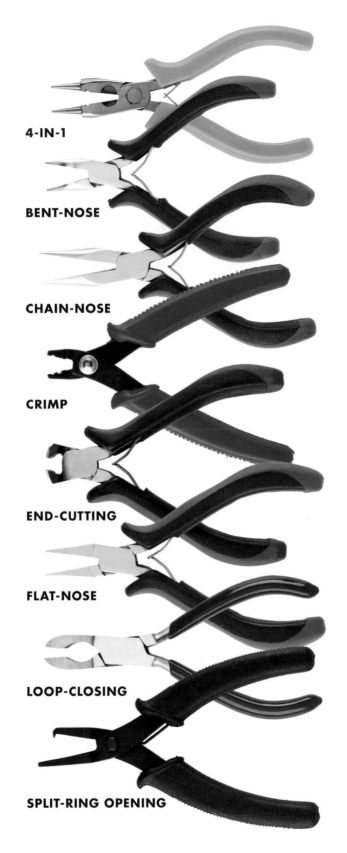

4-IN-1

BENT-NOSE

CHAIN-NOSE

CRIMP

END-CUTTING

FLAT-NOSE

LOOP-CLOSING

SPLIT-RING OPENING

Beading Basics How-to Guide

MAKE YOUR OWN BASIC CLASP

- Cut a 2-inch piece of 18-gauge wire. Use your round-nose pliers or a 4-in-1 tool to grasp the very end of the wire and roll toward you until the wire touches itself (*see Photo A*). You may have to stop part of the way through to adjust your pliers and complete the roll. The loop will now look like a letter P.

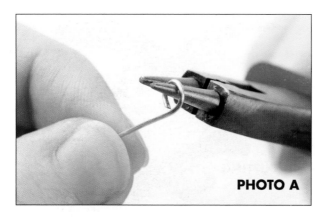

PHOTO A

- Next, form the wire into a hook shape (*see Photo B*).

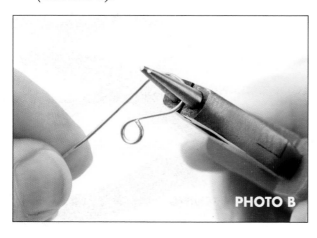

PHOTO B

- To finish your clasp, form a small metal spiral on the other end (*see Photo C*). Grasp the very end of the wire with your round-nose pliers. Roll toward you until the wire touches itself. You may have to stop part of the way through to adjust your pliers and complete the loop.

- Grasp the flat loop with the jaws of your flat-nose pliers, with the end facing out of the pliers. Use your thumb to press the wire tight against itself, forming the beginning of the spiral. Adjust the pliers and continue to press the wire into the spiral (*see Photo C*). Stop when the spiral is the correct size. Tap with a jewelry hammer to strengthen the clasp. Use a jump ring to attach your project (*see Photo D*).

PHOTO C

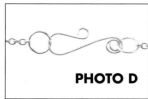

PHOTO D

BEAD CAPS

Bead caps can be used with a bead to create a dangle or can be strung between beads for a totally different look. To create a dangle, use a head pin.

CRIMPING

METHOD 1: 4-IN-1 TOOL

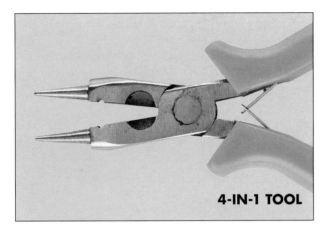

4-IN-1 TOOL

- With the round-nose pliers of your 4-in-1 tool, grab the crimp bead.

- Squeeze gently to flatten the crimp bead.

METHOD 2: CRIMP TOOL

CRIMP TOOL

- Place the crimp bead in the bottom jaw of the crimp pliers.

- Gently squeeze. This will make the crimp C-shaped *(see Photo E)*.

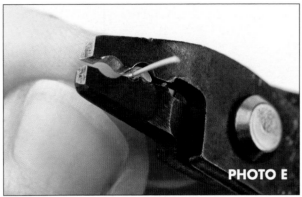

PHOTO E

- Turn the crimp bead 90 degrees counterclockwise and place in the top jaw. It will look like a smile in a set of parentheses *(see Photo F)*.

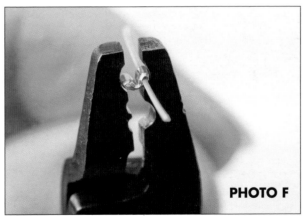

PHOTO F

- Gently squeeze until the bead's two sides have come together.

CRIMP COVERS

- Place the crimp cover in the front opening of your crimp pliers.

- Place the cover around the crimped bead *(see Photo G)*.

- Gently squeeze the pliers to close the crimp cover. Don't press down too hard or you will flatten the crimp cover. Trim excess.

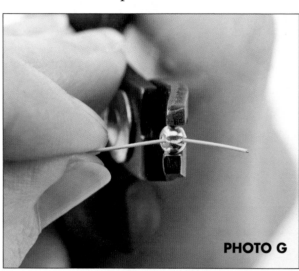

PHOTO G

OPENING & CLOSING JUMP RINGS

- Hold one half of the loop with the opening at the top.

- With 4-in-1 tool, grasp opposite side of loop and twist *(see Photo H)*.

- To close, twist back.

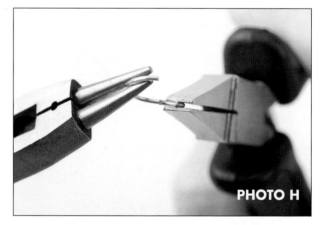

PHOTO H

MAKING YOUR OWN JUMP RINGS

- Use a smooth, round 2–6mm cylinder on your wire-wrapping pliers. Wrap the wire tightly and smoothly around the cylinder *(see Photo I)*.

- Slide the coil off the cylinder.

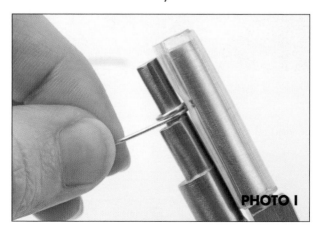

PHOTO I

- Use side-cutting pliers or wire cutters to cut up the center of the coil, forming individual jump rings *(see Photo J)*.

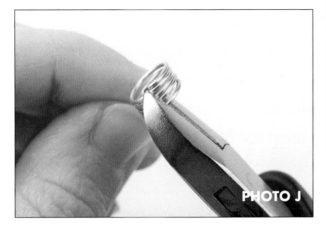

PHOTO J

PHOTO L

- Flattening crimp beads with round-nose pliers *(see Photo M)*.

4-IN-1 PLIERS

This tool is named because of its four functions:

- Manipulating wire with the round-nose pliers *(see Photo K and L)*.

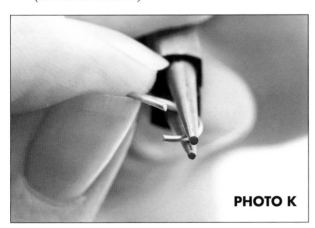

PHOTO K

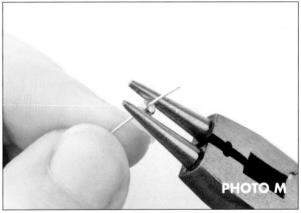

PHOTO M

- Closing loops with the grooves in between the pliers and the cutter *(see Photo N)*.

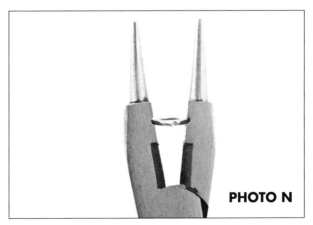

PHOTO N

- Cutting with the cutter.

KNOTS

OVERHAND KNOT

Make a loop and pass the cord behind the loop
and over the front cord. Pull to tighten.

Overhand Knot

SQUARE KNOT

Make one overhand knot, passing the right
cord over the left. Repeat overhand knot,
this time passing left end over right.
Pull to tighten.

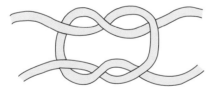

Square Knot

SURGEON'S KNOT

Make one overhand knot, passing the right
cord over the left. Repeat overhand knot,
this time passing left end over right twice.
Pull to tighten.

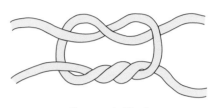

Surgeon's Knot

LARK'S HEAD KNOT

Fold stringing material in half and pass the
folded end through the loop through which
you are attaching the cord. Pull ends of cord
through the loop made at the fold to tighten.

Lark's Head Knot

SIMPLE LOOPS

- Use your round-nose pliers to grasp the very end of the wire. Roll the wire until it touches itself. You may have to stop part of the way through to adjust your pliers and complete the roll. The loop will now look like a letter P (*see Photo O*).

PHOTO O

- Insert the pliers into the loop and use your thumb to reposition the loop into more of a lollipop shape.

TIP To make multiple loops the same size, use a marker to note the position of your loop on the round-nose pliers (*see Photo P*).

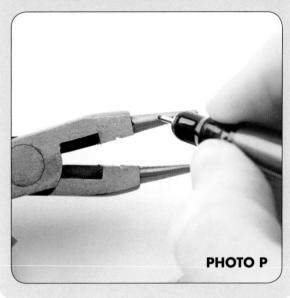

PHOTO P

Black & Silver Affair

NECKLACE

SKILL LEVEL

INTERMEDIATE

FINISHED SIZE
21 inches

MATERIALS
- Size 20 crochet cotton:
  1 ball each black and white
- Doughnut-shape pendant
- Differently shaped black glass
  cabachon beads: 3
- 10/0 or 11/0 seed beads: 50g to 100g of each
  black, silver and argent silver
- Silver cone-shaped bead caps: 8
- Jump rings: 8
- Crimp beads: 16
- Clasp: T or S-hook
- Clasps: 4
- 20 gauge silver jewelry wire
- Silver chain
- Size 11/1.10mm steel crochet hook
- Beading needle
- 4-in-1 pliers
- Beeswax
- Jewelry glue

PATTERN NOTES
Please read all information at the beginning
of this book.

Chain 1 more chain than beads in sequence.
The extra chain is used for joining ring only.

Work in continuous rounds, do not join unless
otherwise stated.

Apply beeswax to crochet cotton before
stringing on beads.

SPECIAL STITCH
Bead slip stitch (bead sl st): Insert hook in
back lp *(see Stitch Guide)* of ch or st as indicated
(see photos on page 4), pull up bead, yo, pull lp
through ch or st and lp on hook.

INSTRUCTIONS
NECKLACE
PENDANT
Cut 42-inch piece of wire. Leaving 3 inches at
top, wrap wire around the Pendant, beg wrap

This necklace may be worn with or without detachable bead strands.

through hole in center, make first lp at top to beg by wrapping wire around shank of crochet hook, twist crochet hook 2 or 3 times, remove hook, [wrap wire around Pendant for another ¼ to ½ inch from last lp at top, make lp with crochet hook] 4 times. Wrap wire as desired and as shown in photo, making 3 lps at bottom 1 inch apart.

Bring wire back to top at first lp, cut wire and wrap end around bottom of first lp.

Wire wrapping doesn't have to be perfect as this adds to the design and gives a place to anchor additions. It also serves as a nice centerpiece for the Necklace.

BOTTOM BEAD DANGLES

1. Thread 1 black glass bead and 25 seed beads on black crochet cotton.

2. Run crochet cotton through bottom center lp on Pendant and back through all beads. Tie 1 or 2 knots in end.

3. Cut crochet cotton, leaving enough to thread through crimp bead.

4. Thread crimp bead right underneath the black glass bead and use pliers to squeeze crimp bead shut. Trim excess crochet cotton.

5. Rep steps 1–4, attaching Dangle to Pendant on each side of first Dangle.

NECK PIECE
MAKE 2.

Getting started: Apply beeswax to crochet cotton. Thread 610 seed beads onto white crochet cotton in the following sequence: argent silver, black, silver, black, argent silver. The sequence of 5 beads will make the pattern.

BEAD TUBE

Rnd 1: Ch 6, sl st in 6th ch from hook to form ring, working in **back lps** (see Stitch Guide), **bead sl st** (see Special Stitch) in back lp of each ch around, **do not join** (see Pattern Notes). (5 bead sl sts)

Rnd 2: Insert hook in same st as first bead, *pull up bead, making sure crochet cotton is in front of previous-row bead and keeping both beads to right of hook, yo, pull through st and lp on hook**, insert hook in next st with bead, rep from * around, ending last rep at **.

Rnds 3–122: Rep rnd 2.

Rnd 123: To make last rnd of beads stand up, sl st in each st around. Fasten off.

BEAD STRANDS
MAKE 2.

1. Using black crochet cotton, bead 4 strands of black seed beads and 1 strand of silver seed beads, making strands 9 inches in length; be sure to leave long ends at each end.

2. Tie knot in each end. Place crimp bead over each knot, and with pliers, squeeze bead closed.

3. Holding 4 strands of black seed beads and 1 strand of silver beads tog, thread ends into 1 bead cap, over jump ring and back through bead cap. Tie ends in knot and trim excess crochet cotton.

4. Place a drop of glue in bead cap and pull cap down over ends of strands.

5. Rep steps 3 and 4 on the rem end.

6. Attach clasp on the jump rings that are on the end of each piece.

You can wear necklace with or without these extra strands.

ASSEMBLY

1. Using crochet cotton on 1 end of Neck Piece, thread end through 1 bead cap, over 1 jump ring and back through bead cap. Run needle back and forth several times through end of Bead Tube to secure end. Trim end closely.

2. Place a drop of glue in bead cap and pull cap down over end of crochet cotton. Cut excess crochet cotton.

3. Rep steps 1 and 2 on other end of Neck Piece.

4. Attach jump rings at ends to clasps on end of 1 Bead Strand.

5. Rep steps 1–4 on rem Neck Piece.

6. Attach jump ring at 1 end of both Neck Pieces and to center lp at top of Pendant.

7. Cut 2 pieces of chain with 3 links each, or the desired amount.

8. Attach jump ring at other end of each Neck Piece to 1 end of each chain-link piece.

9. Attach jump ring to rem end of each chain-link piece.

10. Attach T-hook or S-hook clasp to jump rings at ends of chain links.

BRACELET

SKILL LEVEL

INTERMEDIATE

FINISHED SIZE
6 inches, excluding chain links

MATERIALS
- Size 20 crochet cotton:
  1 ball each black and white
- 10/0 or 11/0 seed beads:
  50g to 100g of each black, silver and argent silver
- 3-hole crystal spacers by Swavorski: 3
- Jump rings: 6
- Crimp beads: 4
- Silver cone-shaped bead caps: 4
- Clasp
- Silver chain
- Size 11/1.10mm steel crochet hook
- Beading needle
- Embroidery needle
- 4-in-1 pliers
- Beeswax
- Jewelry glue

PATTERN NOTES
Please read all information at the beginning of this book.

Chain 1 more chain than beads in sequence. The extra chain is used for joining ring only.

Work in continuous rounds, do not join unless otherwise stated.

SPECIAL STITCH
Bead slip stitch (bead sl st): Insert hook in **back lp** (*see Stitch Guide*) of ch or st as indicated (*see photos on page 4*), pull up bead, yo, pull lp through ch or st and lp on hook.

INSTRUCTIONS
BRACELET
CENTER BEAD TUBE
MAKE 2.
Getting started: Apply beeswax to crochet cotton. Thread 200 seed beads onto white crochet cotton in the following sequence: argent silver, black, silver, black, argent silver. The sequence of 5 beads will make the pattern.

Rnd 1: Ch 6, sl st in 6th ch from hook to form ring, working in **back lps** (*see Stitch Guide*), **bead sl st** (*see Special Stitch*) in back lp of each ch around, **do not join** (*see Pattern Notes*). (*5 bead sl sts*)

Rnd 2: Insert hook in same st as first bead, *pull up bead, making sure crochet cotton is in front of previous-row bead and keeping both beads to right of hook, yo, pull through st and lp on hook**, insert hook in next st with bead, rep from * around, ending last rep at **.

Rnds 3–40: Rep rnd 2.

Rnd 41: To make last rnd of beads stand up, sl st in each st around. Leaving 6- to 8-inch end, fasten off.

OUTSIDE BEAD TUBE
MAKE 4.
Getting started: Apply beeswax to crochet cotton. Thread 210 seed beads onto black crochet cotton in the following sequence: 2 black, silver, 2 black. The sequence of 5 beads will make the pattern.

Rnds 1–40: Rep rnds 1–40 of Center Bead Tube.

Rnds 41 & 42: Rep rnd 2.

Rnd 43: To make last rnd of beads stand up,

sl st in each st around. Leaving 6- to 8-inch end, fasten off.

SPACERS

1. Thread 1 long end of 1 Center Bead Tube in embroidery needle. Insert needle through center hole on Spacer and back through 1 side hole. Pull tight so beads are right up next to Spacer. Run needle back and forth several times through end of Bead Tube to secure end. Trim end closely.

2. Rep step 2 with rem Center Bead Tube on other side of same Spacer.

3. Thread 1 long end of 1 Outside Bead Tube in embroidery needle, insert needle through 1 side hole on Spacer and back through center hole on Spacer. Pull tight so beads are right up next to Spacer. Run needle back and forth several times through end of Bead Tube to secure end. Trim end closely.

4. Rep step 4 on opposite side of Spacer.

5. Rep steps 4 and 5 with rem 2 Outside Bead Tubes.

6. Attach end Spacers in same manner as center Spacer, working on just 1 side of Spacer as shown in photo; be sure to leave enough crochet cotton to attach bead caps to end Spacers.

ASSEMBLY

1. To attach bead caps, run 2 crochet cotton ends *(see step 7 of Spacers)* through bead cap, over jump ring and back through bead cap; do this a few times to tighten cap down to Spacer.

2. Attach other bead cap with rem crochet cotton ends *(see step 7 of Spacers)*. Rep on other end.

3. Separate 5 links of silver chain and attach each end to jump rings on 1 end of Bracelet.

4. Attach 1 end of clasp to center link of 5-chain length.

5. Rep step 4 on rem end of Bracelet.

6. Attach another 7 or desired length of silver chain to center chain of 5 chain links.

7. Attach rem end of clasp to end chain. ■

Colors of Autumn

NECKLACE

SKILL LEVEL

INTERMEDIATE

FINISHED SIZE
17 inches

MATERIALS
- Size 10 crochet cotton:
  1 ball white
- Orange-gold glass pendant
- Medium orange-gold glass beads:
  2 diamond-shape
  2 pear-shape
- 6/0 seed beads:
  50g brown mix
- 3mm seed beads:
  10g gold-plated
- 10/0 seed beads:
  10g each gold and bronze
- Size 7/1.65mm steel crochet hook
- Jump rings: 3
- Gold filigree bead caps: 2
- Gold head pins: 5
- Gold toggle clasp
- Clasps: 4
- Beading needle
- Embroidery needle
- 4-in-1 pliers
- Beeswax
- Jewelry glue

PATTERN NOTES
Please read all information at the beginning of this book.

Chain 1 more chain than beads in sequence. The extra chain is used for joining ring only.

Work in continuous rounds, do not join unless otherwise stated.

SPECIAL STITCH
Bead slip stitch (bead sl st): Insert hook in **back lp** (*see Stitch Guide*) of ch or st as indicated (*see photos on page 4*), pull up bead, yo, pull lp through ch or st and lp on hook.

INSTRUCTIONS
NECKLACE
Getting started: Apply beeswax to crochet cotton. Thread 685 beads onto crochet cotton in the following sequence: brown mix, brown mix, 3mm, brown mix, brown mix. The sequence of 5 beads will make the pattern.

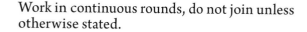

BEAD TUBE

Rnd 1: Ch 6, sl st in 6th ch from hook to form ring, working in **back lps** (*see Stitch Guide*), **bead sl st** (*see Special Stitch*) in back lp of each ch around, **do not join** (*see Pattern Notes*). (*5 bead sl sts*)

Rnd 2: Insert hook in same st as first bead, *pull up bead, making sure crochet cotton is in front of previous-row bead and keeping both beads to right of hook, yo, pull through st and lp on hook**, insert hook in next st with bead, rep from * around, ending last rep at **.

Rnds 3–137: Rep rnd 2.

Rnd 138: To make last rnd of beads stand up, sl st in each st around. Fasten off.

ASSEMBLY

1. Using embroidery needle and crochet cotton on 1 end of Bead Tube, thread end through bead cap, over jump ring and back through bead cap. Run needle back and forth several times through end of Bead Tube to secure end. Trim end closely.

2. Place a drop of glue in bead cap and pull cap down over end of crochet cotton. Cut excess crochet cotton.

3. Rep steps 1 and 2 on other end of Bead Tube.

4. Attach toggle clasp to ends.

CENTER PENDANT

1. Attach jump ring to glass pendant; using head pin with lp on end, attach same jump ring to pin.

2. With pliers, form lp on other end of pin (*see instructions for Simple Loops on page 21*). Attach the lp just made to the center of Necklace.

SIDE PENDANTS

1. Thread 1 diamond-shape bead onto head pin, then 3 bronze, 3 gold and 3 bronze 10/0 seed beads, make lp (*see Simple Loops on page 21*) at top of head pin and attach to Necklace 1 inch from Center Pendant. Rep with rem diamond-shape bead.

2. Rep step 1 with pear-shaped beads, placing 1 on each side of diamond-shape beads.

RING

SKILL LEVEL

INTERMEDIATE

FINISHED SIZE
2¼ inches across

MATERIALS
- Size 20 crochet cotton: 1 ball gold
- Round tiger's-eye bead
- 6/0 seed beads: 50g brown mix
- 3mm seed beads: 100g gold-plated
- 10/0 seed beads: 50g bronze and gold
- Elite Better Beads gold-color metal noodle spacers: 2
- Jolee 2-hole square-shape gold spacers with crystal: 2
- Jump rings: 3
- Gold crimp beads: 4
- .5mm stretch cord
- Size 12/1.00mm steel crochet hook
- Beading needle
- Embroidery needle
- 4-in-1 pliers
- Beeswax
- Jewelry glue

PATTERN NOTES
Please read all information at the beginning of this book.

Join with slip stitch as indicated unless otherwise stated.

Chain-3 at beginning of round counts as first double crochet unless otherwise stated.

SPECIAL STITCHES
Bead single crochet (bead sc): Insert hook in **back lp** (*see Stitch Guide*) of st as indicated (*see photos on page 4*), pull up bead, yo, pull through st, yo, pull through all lps on hook.

Bead double crochet (bead dc): Yo, insert hook in back lp of st as indicated, pull up bead (*see photos on page 5*), yo, pull through st and first lp on hook, pull up bead, yo, pull through last 2 lps on hook.

INSTRUCTIONS
RING
FLOWER
MIDDLE SECTION
Getting started: Apply beeswax to crochet cotton. Thread 200 brown mix seed beads onto crochet cotton.

Row 1: Ch 25, dc in 5th ch from hook (*first 4 chs count as first dc and ch-1*), dc in same ch. Ch 1, sk next ch, (dc, ch 1, dc) in next ch, [ch 1, sk next st, (dc, ch 1, dc) in next ch] across, turn. (*20 ch sps*)

Row 2: Pull up bead, ch 1, pull up bead (*first 2 beads count as first bead dc*), ch 1, 4 **bead dc** (*see Special Stitches*) in first ch sp, 5 bead dc in each ch sp across. Fasten off.

Set this piece aside.

CENTER SECTION
Getting started: Apply beeswax to crochet cotton. Thread 20 gold seed beads onto crochet cotton.

Rnd 1: Ch 11, sl st in first ch to form ring, ch 1, sk first ch, sc in each ch around, **join** (*see Pattern Notes*) in beg sc. (*10 sc*)

Rnd 2: Ch 1, 2 **bead sc** (*see Special Stitches*) in each st around, join in beg sc. Fasten off.

Sew tiger's-eye bead in center of this piece.

Set this piece aside.

FOUNDATION
Getting started: Apply beeswax to crochet cotton. Thread 320 gold seed beads onto crochet cotton.

Rnd 1: Ch 6, sl st in first ch to form ring, ch 1, 2 sc in each ch around, join in beg sc. (*12 sc*)

Rnd 2: **Ch 3** (*see Pattern Notes*), dc in same st, 2 dc in each st around, join in 3rd ch of beg ch-3. (*24 dc*)

Rnds 3 & 4: Rep rnd 2. (*96 dc at end of last rnd*)

Rnd 5: Ch 3, dc in same st, 2 dc in next st, dc in next st, [2 dc in each of next 2 sts, dc in next st] around, join in 3rd ch of beg ch-3. (*160 dc*)

Rnd 6: Pull up bead, ch 1, pull up bead, ch 1, bead dc in each st around, join in 2nd ch of beg ch-2. Fasten off.

ASSEMBLY
1. With Foundation bead side facing you, sew the Middle Section around to rnds 3–5.

2. Sew Center Section in center of Foundation.

3. Cut large enough piece of stretch cord to work with. Fold stretch cord in half, slide 1 crimp bead up, leaving small lp at end to attach Flower. Close crimp bead (*see Page 17*) with pliers.

4. Slide 1 square-shape spacer onto ends of stretch cord up against crimp bead.

5. Slide 1 gold bead, 1 noodle spacer and 1 gold bead onto each end of stretch cord up against square spacer.

6. Slide rem square spacer onto stretch cord. Slide crimp bead onto both ends up close to spacer.

7. Tie surgeon's knot (*see Knots on page 20*) in end of the pieces you have just assembled. Place a drop of glue onto surgeon's knot, keep a lp pulled and close crimp bead.

8. Sew lps at ends to back of Flower with about 1 inch of space between ends. ∎

Flower Vine Set

NECKLACE & BRACELET

SKILL LEVEL

INTERMEDIATE

FINISHED SIZES
Necklace: 24 inches
Bracelet: 11½ inches

MATERIALS
- Size 30 crochet cotton:
  1 ball black
- 14-inch strands red 10/0 seed beads: 18
- 10/0 seed beads:
  100g black
- 3-loop silver spacers: 4
- Jump rings: 4
- Gold toggle clasp
- Toggle clasps: 2
- Silver chain
- Size 12/1.00mm steel crochet hook
- Beading needle
- Embroidery needle
- 4-in-1 pliers
- Beeswax
- Jewelry glue

PATTERN NOTES
Please read all information at the beginning
of this book.

Chain 1 more chain than beads in sequence.
The extra chain is used for joining ring only.

Work in continuous rounds, do not join unless
otherwise stated.

SPECIAL STITCH
Bead slip stitch (bead sl st): Insert hook in
back lp *(see Stitch Guide)* of ch or st as indicated
(see photos on page 4), pull up bead, yo, pull lp
through ch or st and lp on hook.

NECKLACE INSTRUCTIONS
BLACK SHORT STRAND
Getting started: Apply beeswax to crochet
cotton. Thread 1,200 black beads onto
crochet cotton.

BEAD TUBE
Rnd 1: Ch 6, sl st in 6th ch from hook to form
ring, working in **back lps** *(see Stitch Guide)*,
bead sl st *(see Special Stitch)* in back lp of each
ch around, **do not join** *(see Pattern Notes)*.
(5 bead sl sts)

Rnd 2: Insert hook in same st as first bead,

*pull up bead, making sure crochet cotton is in front of previous-row bead and keeping both beads to right of hook, yo, pull through st and lp on hook**, insert hook in next st with bead, rep from * around, ending last rep at **.

Rnds 3–240: Rep rnd 2.

Rnd 241: To make last rnd of beads stand up, sl st in each st around. Fasten off.

BLACK LONG STRAND

Getting started: Apply beeswax to crochet cotton. Thread 1,500 black beads onto crochet cotton.

BEAD TUBE

Rnds 1 & 2: Rep rnds 1 and 2 of Black Short Strand.

Rnds 3–300: Rep rnd 2.

Rnd 301: To make last rnd of beads stand up, sl st in each st around. Fasten off.

RED & BLACK STRAND

Getting started: Apply beeswax to crochet cotton. Thread 1,345 beads onto crochet cotton in sequence as follows: *20 black, 1 red, 3 black, 1 red (*25 seed beads on crochet cotton*), 2 red, 1 black, 12 red, 1 black, 3 red, 3 black, 1 red, 2 black (*50 seed beads on crochet cotton*), 20 black, 1 red, 3 black, 1 red (*75 seed beads on crochet cotton*), 2 red, 1 black, 12 red, 1 black, 3 red, 3 black, 1 red, 2 black (*100 seed beads on crochet cotton*), rep from * until you have all 1,345 beads on crochet cotton.

BEAD TUBE

Rnds 1 & 2: Rep rnds 1 and 2 of Black Short Strand.

Rnds 3–269: Rep rnd 2.

Rnd 270: To make last rnd of beads stand up, sl st in each st around. Fasten off.

ASSEMBLY

1. Thread 1 end of Black Short Strand in embroidery needle. Thread through top lp on 1 spacer bar several times. Run needle several times through end of Black Short Strand to secure. Trim end. Rep with rem end in another spacer bar.

2. Attach Red and Black Strand in center lp of same spacer bars in same manner as Black Short Strand.

3. Attach Black Long Strand to bottom lp of same spacer bars in same manner as Black Short Strand.

4. Attach jump ring to top of spacer bar at each end. Attach 14 chs or desired length of ch to jump ring on 1 end.

5. Attach 4 chs or desired length of ch to jump ring at other end. Attach toggle-clasp to chain.

BRACELET INSTRUCTIONS
BLACK STRAND
MAKE 2.

Getting started: Apply beeswax to crochet cotton. Thread 400 black beads onto crochet cotton.

BEAD TUBE

Rnds 1 & 2: Rep rnds 1 and 2 of Black Short Strand.

Rnds 3–80: Rep rnd 2.

Rnd 81: To make last rnd of beads stand up, sl st in each st around. Fasten off.

RED & BLACK STRAND

Getting started: Apply beeswax to crochet cotton. Thread 400 beads onto crochet cotton in sequence as follows: *20 black, 1 red, 3 black, 1 red (*25 seed beads on crochet cotton*), 2 red, 1 black, 12 red, 1 black, 3 red, 3 black, 1 red, 2 black (*50 seed beads on crochet cotton*), 20 black, 1 red, 3 black, 1 red (*75 seed beads on crochet cotton*), 2 red, 1 black, 12 red, 1 black, 3 red, 3 black, 1 red, 2 black (*100 seed beads on crochet cotton*), rep from * until you have all 400 beads on crochet cotton. The sequence of 5 beads will make the pattern.

BEAD TUBE

Rnds 1 & 2: Rep rnds 1 and 2 of Black Short Strand

Rnds 3–80: Rep rnd 2.

Rnd 81: To make last rnd of beads stand up, sl st in each st around. Fasten off.

ASSEMBLY

1. Rep steps 1–3 of Assembly on Necklace, attaching Black Strand to top lp, Red & Black Strand to center lp and rem Black Strand to bottom lp of spacer bars.

2. Rep steps 4 and 5 of Assembly on Necklace, using 4 or 5 chains on end with toggle clasp and 3 on rem end.

BROACH

SKILL LEVEL

INTERMEDIATE

FINISHED SIZE
4½ inches across

MATERIALS
- Size 30 crochet cotton:
  1 ball each black and red
- Black faceted bead
- 11/0 seed beads: 50g black
- 14-inch strands 10/0 red seed beads: 18
- 9/0 seed beads: 50g black
- Size 7/1.65mm steel crochet hook
- 1-inch pin back
- Beading needle
- Embroidery needle
- 4-in-1 tool
- Beeswax
- Jewelry glue

PATTERN NOTES
Please read all information at the beginning of this book.

Join with slip stitch as indicated unless otherwise stated.

Chain-3 at beginning of row or round counts as first double crochet unless otherwise stated.

SPECIAL STITCHES

Bead slip stitch (bead sl st): Insert hook in back lp of ch or st as indicated (*see photos on page 4*), pull up bead, yo, pull lp through ch or st and lp on hook.

Bead single crochet (bead sc): Insert hook in back lp of st as indicated (*see photos on page 4*), pull up bead, yo, pull through st, yo, pull through all lps on hook.

Bead half double crochet (bead hdc): Yo, insert hook in back lp of st as indicated (*see photos on page 5*), pull up bead, yo, pull through st and 2 lps on hook.

Bead double crochet (bead dc): Yo, insert hook in back lp of st as indicated, pull up bead (*see photos on page 5*), yo, pull through st and first lp on hook, pull up bead, yo, pull through last 2 lps on hook.

Bead double double crochet (bead double dc): Yo 3 times, insert hook in back lp of st as indicated, pull up bead (*see photos on page 6*), yo, pull through st and first lp on hook, [pull up bead, yo, pull through 2 lps on hook] 3 times.

V-stitch (V-st): (Dc, ch 1, dc) as indicated in instructions.

INSTRUCTIONS
SMALL LEAF
MAKE 7.
Getting started: Apply beeswax to crochet cotton. Thread 88 red seed beads onto black crochet cotton.

Ch 18, **bead sc** (*see Special Stitches*) in 2nd ch from hook, **bead hdc** (*see Special Stitches*) in next ch, **bead dc** (*see Special Stitches*) in each of next 3 chs, **bead double dc** (*see Special Stitches*) in each of next 7 chs, bead dc in each of next 3 chs, bead hdc in next st, bead sc in last ch, working on opposite side of ch, ch 3, bead sc in next ch, bead hdc in next ch, bead dc in each of next 3 chs, bead double dc in each of next 7 chs, bead dc in each of next 3 chs, bead hdc in next ch, bead sc in last ch.

LARGE LEAF
MAKE 7

Getting Started: Use beeswax on crochet cotton. Thread 140 red seed beads onto black crochet cotton.

Rnd 1: Ch 18, bead sc in 2nd ch from hook, bead hdc in next ch, bead dc in each of next 3 chs, bead double dc in each of next 7 chs, bead dc in each of next 3 chs, bead hdc in next st, bead sc in last ch, working on opposite side of ch, ch 3, bead sc in next ch, bead hdc in next ch, bead dc in each of next 3 chs, bead double dc in each of next 7 chs, bead dc in each of next 3 chs, bead hdc in next ch, bead sc in last ch.

Rnd 2: Bead sl st (*see Special Stitches*) in each of next 6 sts, ch 1, bead sc in each of next 2 sts, bead dc in each of next 2 sts, bead double dc in next st, bead dc in each of next 3 sts, bead hdc in next st, bead sc in last st, bead sl st in next st, bead sl st in each of next 3 chs, bead sl st in next st, bead sc in each of next 2 sts, bead hdc in next st, bead dc in each of next 2 sts, bead double dc in next st, bead dc in each of next 2 sts, bead sc in each of next 2 sts, bead sl st in each st around. Fasten off.

FOUNDATION

Rnd 1: With black, ch 4, sl st in first ch to form ring, ch 1, 8 sc in ring, **join** (*see Pattern Notes*) in beg sc. (*8 sc*)

Rnd 2: Ch 1, 2 sc in each st around, join in beg sc. (*16 sc*)

Rnd 3: Rep rnd 2. (*32 sc*)

Rnd 4: Ch 1, sc in each st around, join.

Rnd 5: Rep rnd 2. (*64 sc*)

Rnds 6–8: **Ch 3** (*see Pattern Notes*), dc in each st around, join in 3rd ch of beg ch-3.

Rnd 9: Ch 3, dc in same st, 2 dc in each st around, join in 3rd ch of beg ch-3. Fasten off. (*128 dc*)

CENTER B

Getting started: Apply beeswax to crochet cotton. Thread 200 9/0 black beads onto black crochet cotton.

Rnd 1: Ch 24, **V-st** (*see Special Stitches*) in 5th ch from hook, [ch 1, sk next ch, V-st in next ch] across, turn. (*20 V-sts*)

Rnd 2: Sl st in first ch sp, (pull up bead, ch 1) twice (*counts as first bead dc*), 4 bead dc in same ch sp, 5 bead dc in each ch sp around. Fasten off.

Set this piece aside.

CENTER A

Getting started: Apply beeswax to crochet cotton. Thread 200 11/0 black seed beads onto red crochet cotton.

Rnds 1 & 2: Rep rnds 1 and 2 of Center B.

ASSEMBLY

1. Sew ⅓ of end of rows on Large Leaves to last rnd of Foundation.

2. Sew Small Leaves between Large Leaves.

3. Sew Center B to Foundation next and Center A in rem center of Foundation. Sew facete bead in center of Center A.

4. Sew pin back to back of Foundation. ∎

Shades of Nature

SKILL LEVEL

INTERMEDIATE

FINISHED SIZES
Necklace: 26 inches
Earrings: 3½ inches

MATERIALS
- Size 30 crochet cotton:
  1 ball white
- 10/0 seed beads: 100g silver
- 14-inch strands 10/0 opaque seed beads:
  18 red
  18 turquoise
- 1-inch round findings with 5 eyes: 2 silver
- ⅜-inch round findings with 3 eyes: 2 silver
- Fishhook ear wires: 2
- Silver toggle clasp
- Jump rings: 4
- Crimp beads: 6
- Silver chain
- Size 12/1.00mm steel crochet hook
- Beading needle
- Embroidery needle
- 4-in-1 pliers
- Beeswax
- Jewelry glue

PATTERN NOTES
Please read all information at the beginning
of this book.

Chain 1 more chain than beads in sequence.
The extra chain is used for joining ring only.

Work in continuous rounds, do not join unless
otherwise stated.

SPECIAL STITCH
Bead slip stitch (bead sl st): Insert hook in
back lp (*see Stitch Guide*) of ch or st as indicated (*see photos on page 4*), pull up bead, yo,
pull lp through ch or st and lp on hook.

NECKLACE INSTRUCTIONS
SHORT SILVER STRAND
Getting started: Apply beeswax to crochet
cotton. Thread 777 silver seed beads onto
crochet cotton.

BEAD TUBE

Rnd 1: Ch 4, sl st in 4th ch from hook to form ring, working in **back lps** (see Stitch Guide), **bead sl st** (see Special Stitch) in back lp of each ch around, **do not join** (see Pattern Notes). (3 bead sl sts)

Rnd 2: Insert hook in same st as first bead, *pull up bead, making sure crochet cotton is in front of previous-row bead and keeping both beads to right of hook, yo, pull through st and lp on hook**, insert hook in next st with bead, rep from * around, ending last rep at **.

Rnds 3–259: Rep rnd 2.

Rnd 260: To make last rnd of beads stand up, sl st in each st around. Fasten off.

MEDIUM SILVER STRAND

Getting started: Apply beeswax to crochet cotton. Thread 876 silver seed beads onto crochet cotton.

BEAD TUBE

Rnd 1: Rep rnd 1 of Short Silver Strand.

Rnds 2–292: Rep rnd 2 of Short Silver Strand.

Rnd 293: Rep rnd 260 of Short Silver Strand.

LONG SILVER STRAND

Getting started: Apply beeswax to crochet cotton. Thread 1,020 silver seed beads onto crochet cotton.

BEAD TUBE

Rnd 1: Rep rnd 1 of Short Silver Strand.

Rnds 2–340: Rep rnd 2 of Short Silver Strand.

Rnd 241: Rep rnd 260 of Short Silver Strand.

SHORT SILVER, TURQUOISE & RED STRAND

Getting started: Apply beeswax to crochet cotton. Thread 1,050 seed beads onto crochet cotton in sequence of: 325 red, [1 silver, 3 red, 1 silver] 25 times, 150 silver, [1 silver, 3 turquoise, 1 silver] 25 times, 325 turquoise. The sequence of 5 beads in [] will make the pattern.

BEAD TUBE

Rnd 1: Ch 6, sl st in 6th ch from hook to form ring, working in back lps, bead sl st in back lp of each ch around, do not join. (5 bead sl sts)

Rnd 2: Insert hook in same st as first bead, *pull up bead, making sure your crochet cotton is in front of previous-row bead and keeping both beads to right of hook, yo, pull through st and lp on hook**, insert hook in next st with bead, rep from * around, ending last rep at **.

Rnds 3–210: Rep rnd 2.

Rnd 211: To make last rnd of beads stand up, sl st in each st around. Fasten off.

LONG SILVER, TURQUOISE & RED STRAND

Getting started: Apply beeswax to crochet cotton. Thread 1,680 seed beads onto crochet cotton in sequence of: 560 turquoise, [1 silver, 3 turquoise, 1 silver] 37 times, 190 silver, [1 silver, 3 red, 1 silver] 37 times, 560 red. The sequence of 5 beads in [] will make the pattern.

BEAD TUBE

Rnd 1: Rep rnd 1 of Short Silver, Turquoise & Red Strand.

Rnds 2–336: Rep rnd 2 of Short Silver, Turquoise & Red Strand.

Rnd 337: Rep rnd 211 of Short Silver, Turquoise & Red Strand.

ASSEMBLY

1. Thread 1 end of Short Silver, Turquoise & Red Strand in embroidery needle, wrap crochet cotton several times in top eye of 1 ring finding with 5 eyes. Run needle back and forth several times through end of Bead Tube to secure. Rep with rem end and rem ring finding.

2. Rep step 1 with Short Silver Strand in next eye on ring findings.

3. Rep step 1 with Medium Silver Strand in next eye on ring findings.

4. Rep step 1 with Long Silver, Turquoise & Red Strand in next eye on ring findings.

5. Rep step 1 with Long Silver Strand in last eye on ring finding.

6. Measure 6 to 7 inches of silver chain for each end.

7. Attach 1 end of each chain piece to jump ring, attach jump ring to ring finding at other end.

8. Attach toggle clasp to ends.

EARRING
MAKE 2.
SILVER STRAND
MAKE 2.

Getting started: Apply beeswax to crochet cotton. Thread 105 silver seed beads onto crochet cotton.

BEAD TUBE

Rnd 1: **Ch 4** *(see Pattern Notes)*, sl st in 4th ch from hook to form ring, working in **back lps** *(see Stitch Guide)*, **bead sl st** *(see Special Stitch)* in back lp of each ch around, **do not join** *(see Pattern Notes)*. *(3 bead sl sts)*

Rnd 2: Insert hook in same st as first bead, *pull up bead, making sure crochet cotton is in front of previous-row bead and keeping both beads to right of hook, yo, pull through st and lp on hook**, insert hook in next st with bead, rep from * around, ending last rep at **.

Rnds 3–35: Rep rnd 2.

Rnd 36: To make last rnd of beads stand up, sl st in each st around. Fasten off.

SILVER, TURQUOISE & RED STRAND

Getting started: Apply beeswax to crochet cotton. Thread 150 beads onto crochet cotton in sequence of: [1 silver, 3 turquoise, 1 silver] 10 times, 50 silver, [1 silver, 3 red, 1 silver] 10 times. The sequence of 5 beads in [ ] will make the pattern.

BEAD TUBE

Rnd 1: Rep rnd 1 of Silver Strand.

Rnds 2–30: Rep rnd 2 of Silver Strand.

Rnd 31: Rep rnd 36 of Silver Strand.

ASSEMBLY

1. Thread 1 end of 1 Silver Strand in embroidery needle, wrap crochet cotton several times in top eye of 1 ring finding with 3 eyes. Run needle back and forth several times through end of Bead Tube to secure.

2. Rep step 1 with Silver, Turquoise & Red Strand in center eye.

3. Rep step 1 with rem Silver Strand in last eye.

4. Attach 1 crimp bead *(see page 17)* to rem end of each Strand.

5. Attach fishhook ear wire to top of each finding. ∎

Chunky Bronzite & Gold

SKILL LEVEL

INTERMEDIATE

FINISHED SIZES
Necklace: 22 inches
Bracelet: 8½ inches

MATERIALS
- Size 20 crochet cotton:
  1 ball gold
- 6/0 beads:
  50g tortoise
- 3mm seed beads:
  10g gold-plated
- Gold filigree bead caps: 8
- Jump rings: 8
- Toggle clasps: 2
- Gold chain
- Size 7/1.65mm steel crochet hook
- Beading needle
- Embroidery needle
- 4-in-1 tool
- Beeswax
- Jewelry glue

PATTERN NOTES
Please read all information at the beginning of this book.

Chain 1 more chain than beads in sequence. The extra chain is used for joining ring only.

Work in continuous rounds, do not join unless otherwise stated.

SPECIAL STITCH
Bead slip stitch (bead sl st): Insert hook in **back lp** (*see Stitch Guide*) of ch or st as indicated (*see photos on page 4*), pull up bead, yo, pull lp through ch or st and lp on hook.

NECKLACE
END
MAKE 2.
Getting started: Apply beeswax to crochet cotton. Thread 175 beads onto crochet cotton in the following sequence: 1 tortoise, 1 gold, 3 tortoise, 1 gold and 1 tortoise. The sequence of 7 beads will make the pattern.

BEAD TUBE

Rnd 1: Ch 8, sl st in 8th ch from hook to form ring, working in **back lps** (see Stitch Guide), **bead sl st** (see Special Stitch) in back lp of each ch around, **do not join** (see Pattern Notes). (7 bead sl sts)

Rnd 2: Insert hook in same st as first bead, *pull up bead, making sure crochet cotton is in front of previous-row bead and keeping both beads to right of hook, yo, pull through st and lp on hook**, insert hook in next st with bead, rep from * around, ending last rep at **.

Rnds 3–25: Rep rnd 2.

Rnd 26: To make last rnd of beads stand up, sl st in each st around. Fasten off.

Place these pieces to side.

CENTER

Getting started: Apply beeswax to crochet cotton. Thread 525 beads onto crochet cotton in the following sequence: 1 tortoise, 1 gold, 3 tortoise, 1 gold and 1 tortoise. The sequence of 7 beads will make the pattern.

BEAD TUBE

Rnd 1: Rep rnd 1 of End.

Rnds 2–75: Rep rnd 2 of End.

Rnd 76: Rep rnd 26 of End.

ASSEMBLY

1. Cut 1 piece of gold chain 10½ inches in length and another 12 inches in length.

2. Thread 1 end of Center through bead cap and over jump ring and 1 end of each piece of gold chain from step 1 and back through bead cap. Run needle back and forth several times through end of Bead Tube to secure. Trim end closely. Place a drop of glue under bead cap and pull tightly down. Rep on rem end of Center.

3. Thread 1 end of 1 End piece through bead cap and jump ring on 1 end of Center and back through bead cap. Run needle back and forth several times through end of Crochet Bead Tube to secure. Trim end closely. Place a drop of glue under bead cap and pull tightly down.

4. Rep step 3 with rem End piece on other end of Center.

5. Thread rem end of 1 End piece through bead cap, jump ring and back through bead cap. Run needle back and forth several times through end of Crochet Bead Tube to secure. Trim end closely. Place a drop of glue under bead cap and pull tightly down. Rep with rem end on other End piece.

6. Cut two 3-inch pieces of gold chain and attach one to each jump ring at end of Ends.

7. Attach toggle clasp to end of 3-inch gold chains.

BRACELET

Getting started: Apply beeswax to crochet cotton. Thread 350 beads onto crochet cotton in the following sequence: 1 tortoise, 1 gold, 3 tortoise, 1 gold and 1 tortoise. The sequence of 7 beads will make the pattern.

BEAD TUBE

Rnd 1: Rep rnd 1 of Necklace End.

Rnds 2–50: Rep rnd 2 of Necklace End.

Rnd 51: Rep rnd 26 of Necklace End.

ASSEMBLY

1. Thread 1 end of Bead Tube through bead cap and jump ring and back through bead cap. Run needle back and forth several times through end of Bead Tube to secure. Trim end closely. Place a drop of glue under bead cap and pull tightly down. Rep with rem end.

2. Attach 5 chain links to jump ring at each end of Bracelet.

3. Attach toggle clasp. ■

Gold & Bronze Set

NECKLACE

SKILL LEVEL

INTERMEDIATE

FINISHED SIZE
42 inches

MATERIALS
- Size 30 crochet cotton:
  1 ball white
- 11/0 seed beads: 30g each bronze and gold
- 3mm seed beads:
  30g gold-plated
- 3 sizes assorted orange-gold leaves with gold eye attached: 18
- Gold filigree bead caps: 6
- Jump rings: 10
- Gold chain
- Size 12/1.00mm steel crochet hook
- Beading needle
- Embroidery needle
- 4-in-1 pliers
- Beeswax
- Jewelry glue

PATTERN NOTES
Please read all information at the beginning of this book.

Chain 1 more chain than beads in sequence. The extra chain is used for joining ring only.

Work in continuous rounds, do not join unless otherwise stated.

SPECIAL STITCH
Bead slip stitch (bead sl st): Insert hook in **back lp** (*see Stitch Guide*) of ch or st as indicated (*see photos on page 4*), pull up bead, yo, pull lp through ch or st and lp on hook.

INSTRUCTIONS
LONG STRAND
Getting started: Apply beeswax to crochet cotton. Thread 2,100 seed beads onto crochet cotton in the following sequence: gold, bronze, gold-plated, bronze, gold; next row: bronze, gold, gold-plated, gold and bronze. The sequence of 5 beads and 2 rows will make the pattern.

BEAD TUBE

Rnd 1: **Ch 6**, sl st in 6th ch from hook to form ring, working in **back lps** (see Stitch Guide), **bead sl st** (see Special Stitch) in back lp of each ch around, **do not join** (see Pattern Notes). (5 bead sl sts)

Rnd 2: Insert hook in same st as first bead, *pull up bead, making sure crochet cotton is in front of previous-row bead and keeping both beads to right of hook, yo, pull through st and lp on hook**, insert hook in next st with bead, rep from * around, ending last rep at **.

Rnds 3–420: Rep rnd 2.

Rnd 421: To make last rnd of beads stand up, sl st in each st around. Fasten off.

SHORT STRAND
MAKE 2.

Getting started: Apply beeswax to crochet cotton. Thread 210 seed beads onto crochet cotton in the following sequence: gold, bronze, gold-plated, bronze, gold; next row: bronze, gold, gold-plated, gold and bronze. The sequence of 5 beads and 2 rows will make the pattern.

BEAD TUBE

Rnds 1 & 2: Rep rnds 1 and 2 of Long Strand.

Rnds 3–42: Rep rnd 2 of Long Strand.

Rnd 43: Rep rnd 421 of Long Strand.

ASSEMBLY

1. Thread 1 end of Long Strand in embroidery needle, thread through bead cap, over jump ring and back through bead cap. Run needle back and forth several times through end of Bead Tube to secure. Trim end closely. Place a drop of glue under bead cap and pull tightly down. Rep on rem end of Long Strand.

2. Thread 1 end of 1 Short Strand in embroidery needle, thread through bead cap, over jump ring on 1 end of Long Strand and back through bead cap. Run needle back and forth several times through end of Bead Tube to secure. Trim end closely. Place a drop of glue under bead cap and pull tightly down. Rep with rem Short Strand on other end of Long Strand.

3. Thread rem end of Short Strand in embroidery needle, thread through bead cap, over jump ring and back through bead cap. Run needle back and forth several times through end of Bead Tube to secure. Trim end closely. Place a drop of glue under bead cap and pull tightly down. Rep with rem end on other Short Strand.

4. Place 3 different-size leaves on each rem jump ring.

5. Cut gold chain into 6 pieces of 3 or 4 links.

6. Attach 1 jump ring with leaves to 1 end of each chain-link piece.

7. Attach 3 chain-link pieces to jump ring at end of each Short Strand.

EARRINGS

 SKILL LEVEL

INTERMEDIATE

FINISHED SIZE
2½ inches

MATERIALS
- Size 30 crochet cotton: 1 ball white
- 11/0 seed beads: 10g each bronze and gold
- 3mm seed beads: 10g gold-plated
- Orange-gold leaves with gold eye attached: 2
- Gold filigree bead caps: 4
- Jump rings: 6
- Fishhook ear wires: 2
- Size 12/1.00mm steel crochet hook
- Beading needle
- Embroidery needle
- 4-in-1 tool
- Beeswax
- Jewelry glue

PATTERN NOTES
Please read all information at the beginning of this book.

Chain 1 more chain than beads in sequence. The extra chain is used for joining ring only.

Work in continuous rounds, do not join unless otherwise stated.

SPECIAL STITCH

Bead slip stitch (bead sl st): Insert hook in **back lp** (*see Stitch Guide*) of ch or st as indicated (*see photos on page 4*), pull up bead, yo, pull lp through ch or st and lp on hook.

EARRING
MAKE 2.

Getting started: Apply beeswax to crochet cotton. Thread 210 beads onto crochet cotton in the following sequence: gold, bronze, gold-plated, bronze, gold; next row: bronze, gold, gold-plated, gold and bronze. The sequence of 5 beads and 2 rows will make the pattern.

BEAD TUBE

Rnd 1: Ch 6, sl st in 6th ch from hook to form ring, working in **back lps** (*see Stitch Guide*), **bead sl st** (*see Special Stitch*) in back lp of each ch around, **do not join** (*see Pattern Notes*). (*5 bead sl sts*)

Rnd 2: Insert hook in same st as first bead, *pull up bead, making sure crochet cotton is in front of previous-row bead and keeping both beads to right of hook, yo, pull through st and lp on hook**, insert hook in next st with bead, rep from * around, ending last rep at **.

Rnds 3–42: Rep rnd 2.

Rnd 43: To make last rnd of beads stand up, sl st in each st around. Fasten off.

ASSEMBLY

1. Thread 1 end in embroidery needle, thread through bead cap, over jump ring and back through bead cap. Run needle back and forth several times through end of Bead Tube to secure. Trim end closely. Place a drop of glue under bead cap and pull tightly down. Rep on rem end of Earring.

2. Fold Earring so ends are tog, attach jump ring to 1 end, to leaf and to other end and to fishhook ear wire. ■

STITCH GUIDE

STITCH ABBREVIATIONS

beg	begin/begins/beginning
bpdc	back post double crochet
bpsc	back post single crochet
bptr	back post treble crochet
CC	contrasting color
ch(s)	chain(s)
ch-	refers to chain or space previously made (i.e., ch-1 space)
ch sp(s)	chain space(s)
cl(s)	cluster(s)
cm	centimeter(s)
dc	double crochet (singular/plural)
dc dec	double crochet 2 or more stitches together, as indicated
dec	decrease/decreases/decreasing
dtr	double treble crochet
ext	extended
fpdc	front post double crochet
fpsc	front post single crochet
fptr	front post treble crochet
g	gram(s)
hdc	half double crochet
hdc dec	half double crochet 2 or more stitches together, as indicated
inc	increase/increases/increasing
lp(s)	loop(s)
MC	main color
mm	millimeter(s)
oz	ounce(s)
pc	popcorn(s)
rem	remain/remains/remaining
rep(s)	repeat(s)
rnd(s)	round(s)
RS	right side
sc	single crochet (singular/plural)
sc dec	single crochet 2 or more stitches together, as indicated
sk	skip/skipped/skipping
sl st(s)	slip stitch(es)
sp(s)	space(s)/spaced
st(s)	stitch(es)
tog	together
tr	treble crochet
trtr	triple treble
WS	wrong side
yd(s)	yard(s)
yo	yarn over

YARN CONVERSION

OUNCES TO GRAMS		GRAMS TO OUNCES	
1	28.4	25	⅞
2	56.7	40	1⅖
3	85.0	50	1¾
4	113.4	100	3½

UNITED STATES		UNITED KINGDOM
sl st (slip stitch)	=	sc (single crochet)
sc (single crochet)	=	dc (double crochet)
hdc (half double crochet)	=	htr (half treble crochet)
dc (double crochet)	=	tr (treble crochet)
tr (treble crochet)	=	dtr (double treble crochet)
dtr (double treble crochet)	=	ttr (triple treble crochet)
skip	=	miss

Single crochet decrease (sc dec): (Insert hook, yo, draw lp through) in each of the sts indicated, yo, draw through all lps on hook.

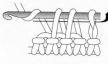

Example of 2-sc dec

Half double crochet decrease (hdc dec): (Yo, insert hook, yo, draw lp through) in each of the sts indicated, yo, draw through all lps on hook.

Example of 2-hdc dec

Reverse single crochet (reverse sc): Ch 1, sk first st, working from left to right, insert hook in next st from front to back, draw up lp on hook, yo, and draw through both lps on hook.

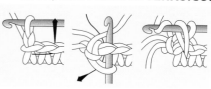

Chain (ch): Yo, pull through lp on hook.

Single crochet (sc): Insert hook in st, yo, pull through st, yo, pull through both lps on hook.

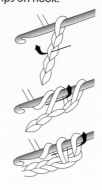

Double crochet (dc): Yo, insert hook in st, yo, pull through st, [yo, pull through 2 lps] twice.

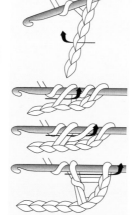

Double crochet decrease (dc dec): (Yo, insert hook, yo, draw lp through, yo, draw through 2 lps on hook) in each of the sts indicated, yo, draw through all lps on hook.

Example of 2-dc dec

Front loop (front lp) Back loop (back lp)

Front Loop   Back Loop

Front post stitch (fp): Back post stitch (bp): When working post st, insert hook from right to left around post of st on previous row.

Back   Front

Post of Stitch

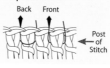

Half double crochet (hdc): Yo, insert hook in st, yo, pull through st, yo, pull through all 3 lps on hook.

Double treble crochet (dtr): Yo 3 times, insert hook in st, yo, pull through st, [yo, pull through 2 lps] 4 times.

Treble crochet decrease (tr dec): Holding back last lp of each st, tr in each of the sts indicated, yo, pull through all lps on hook.

Example of 2-tr dec

Slip stitch (sl st): Insert hook in st, pull through both lps on hook.

Chain color change (ch color change) Yo with new color, draw through last lp on hook.

Double crochet color change (dc color change) Drop first color, yo with new color, draw through last 2 lps of st.

Treble crochet (tr): Yo twice, insert hook in st, yo, pull through st, [yo, pull through 2 lps] 3 times.

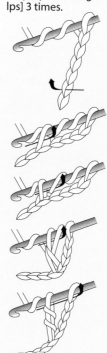

How to Crochet Bead-tube Jewelry is published by DRG, 306 East Parr Road, Berne, IN 46711.
Printed in USA. Copyright © 2011 DRG.

RETAIL STORES: If you would like to carry this pattern book or any other DRG publications, visit DRGwholesale.com

Every effort has been made to ensure that the instructions in this publication are complete and accurate.
We cannot, however, take responsibility for human error, typographical mistakes or variations in individual work.
Please visit AnniesCustomerCare.com to check for pattern updates.

ISBN: 978-1-59635-384-8

1 2 3 4 5 6 7 8 9